# Suri's Burn Book

## WELL-DRESSED COMMENTARY FROM HOLLYWOOD'S LITTLE SWEETHEART

### Allie Hagan

RUNNING PRESS
PHILADELPHIA · LONDON

## DISCLAIMER

**This book is a work of humor. It was not authorized, prepared, approved, licensed, or endorsed by Suri Cruise, or anyone on her behalf, nor does it reflect her actual views—as far as we know.**

Books published by Running Press are available at special discounts for bulk purchases in the United States by corporations, institutions, and other organizations. For more information, please contact the Special Markets Department at the Perseus Books Group, 2300 Chestnut Street, Suite 200, Philadelphia, PA 19103, or call (800) 810-4145, ext. 5000, or e-mail special.markets@perseusbooks.com.

ISBN 978-0-7624-4735-0
Library of Congress Control Number: 2012931369

E-book ISBN 978-0-7624-4750-3

9   8   7   6   5   4   3   2
Digit on the right indicates the number of this printing

Cover and interior design by Amanda Richmond
Edited by Jordana Tusman
Typography: Neutra and HT Gelateria

Running Press Book Publishers
2300 Chestnut Street
Philadelphia, PA 19103-4371

Visit us on the web!
www.runningpress.com
www.surisburnbook.tumblr.com

# Contents

**INTRODUCTION 5**

**PART 1**
**Starting Off Right: Birth in Hollywood 8**
Baby Names 9
Celebrity Twins 14
Celebrities Who Should Have Babies 16
Who's Doing It Right 21

**PART 2**
**Celebrity Dynasties: The Modern-Day Feudal System 24**
Who's Doing It Right 44

**PART 3**
**Dressed to Distress: Celebrity Child Fashion 46**
Suri's Best Fashion Advice 65
Who's Doing It Right 67

**PART 4**

**Old Hollywood Money and the Nouveau Riche:
Social Capital in the Modern Economy 68**

The Celebrity Children I'm Over Already 92

How to Be Old Money 96

Who's Doing It Right 97


**PART 5**

**The Royals: English Nobility and Various
Aristocrats (Like Me) 98**

Who's Doing It Right 106


**PART 6**

**Cliques I'm Not In 108**

Who's Doing It Right 123


Conclusion 124

Acknowledgments 126

Photo Credits 128

# Introduction

*In the celebrity world, most of us wear designer, but only one of us is a legend.*

**A**ND ONLY ONE OF US IS QUALIFIED TO TAKE THE poorly dressed, the poorly behaved, and the just-plain-poor to task, which is what I'm here today to do. If you bought this book expecting a charming tell-all about my Hollywood playground pals, then you're about to be very disappointed. I may count A-list children like Louis Bullock, Willow

Smith, and all four Beckhams among my social acquaintances, but there is no love lost among us.

(Well, except for Cruz Beckham; that's a lost love from which I may never fully recover.)

Yes, Americans are now fully obsessed with celebrity families—as well we should be. We've been slowly building an army of fameworthy children for decades, but when Violet

Affleck, Kingston Rossdale, Shiloh Jolie-Pitt, and a little lady I like to call *moi* were born within a six-month span, the world welcomed a new generation of Hollywood royalty. Oh, gosh, did I just call Violet Affleck fameworthy? Well, let's just say that some children have squandered a great deal of potential.

I'm not afraid to break some confidences, break some spirits, or break some hearts. All's fair in love and war—why else would they have invented the word *frenemy*?

I hope this isn't giving you the impression that I'm elitist or unfriendly. The truth is, I'm terribly nice. I just like things a certain way, and I hold my peers to the same nearly unreachable standard to which I hold myself. When my friends achieve the level of perfection that takes me a team of world-class stylists and a personal lifestyle coach to achieve, I applaud them. Actually, I've only seen that happen a handful of times, but when it does, the only thing I feel is pride.

And, okay, a little jealousy when Reese Witherspoon's daughter Ava pulls off the hipster look without also looking unshowered. Or when Harper Beckham fits into a sample size I *tried* to force myself into. Or when Blue Ivy Carter . . . you get the idea.

The point is, it's only mean when you say it to their faces, right?

My rivalries may be well documented by this point, but never before have they been so detailed, so honest, so *definitive*. Oh, I may find Jessica Alba's daughter Haven a nuisance on Monday, but so often by Tuesday, she's become just another smug baby. For this little project, I've been forced to truly consider my opinions on just about everyone I know. Here you will find the authoritative guide to everyone from Pax Jolie-Pitt to Sasha Obama to Elizabeth McAdams-Gosling. (Okay, I made that last one up. What are you doing with your life, Rachel McAdams?)

So please, have a seat, ask your maid to bring you a cold drink, and enjoy my book.

Except you, Shiloh. I can already tell you're going to hate it.

# PART 1

# Starting Off Right:
# Birth in Hollywood

*Not every birth merits an announcement on the cover of Vanity Fair magazine, but you can do better than a Twitpic.*

**F**ROM THE MOMENT THE BABY BUMP RUMORS start, fame is a make-or-break game for a celebrity child. The hardest part about building one's image in this town is that babies are inherently dependent upon their parents in the beginning. Jessica Simpson's daughter could turn out to be a genuinely lovely person, but she'll never overcome the stigma of having lived inside this.

Sure, not every girl has the privilege

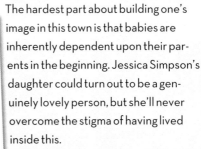

of coming into the world the way I did—shrouded in mystery and poised for greatness—but even C-list celebrities can ensure that their children arrive with a little grace. This chapter will cover some dos and don'ts for starting a baby on the right foot. (Lesson one: Louboutins.)

# BABY NAMES

**THIS IS ONE AREA WHERE FAILURE IS NOT AN OPTION—** children must carry this name around for the rest of their lives. Most celebrities try to give their child a name that will stand out. How many other Knoxes or Seraphinas or Sparrows do you know? Probably not many. But there is a balance to be struck between "unique" and "just plain crazy."

Celebrity chef Jaime Oliver and his wife Jools named their children Poppy Honey Rosie, Daisy Boo Pamela, Petal Blossom Rainbow, and Buddy Bear Maurice. Let me just tell you, the only way Poppy Honey Anything is coming to my tea party is if it's a new expensive blend of Darjeeling. And, I mean, Petal Blossom Rainbow? Good luck getting into college, a country club, or basically anything that isn't a commune. They didn't give you *anything* to work with.

Obviously the most famous A-list child with a too-wacky name is the heiress to the Goop and Coldplay fortune herself, Apple Blythe Alison Martin. Here is what Gwyneth Paltrow says about the meaning behind the name:

"Basically it was because when we were first pregnant, her daddy said, 'If it's a girl, I think her name should be Apple.' And it sounded so sweet, and it conjures such a lovely picture for me. You know apples are so sweet, and they're wholesome, and it's biblical, and I just thought it sounded so lovely and clean, and then I just thought—*perfect*. And then she was born, and it became like an international outrage, which I found surprising because there are people named Rose or Lily or Ivy or June, or you know, lots of pretty nouns."

First of all, "international outrage" is a little bit of revisionist history. When I think of an international outrage, I think of the Cuban Missile Crisis or Iran-Contra or the series finale of *Lost*. Certainly many, many people made fun of Gwyneth and her baby, but no one threatened to deport them or anything. Second of all, I don't care how many contradictory adjectives you put behind it, *Apple* is a terrible name. But like it or not, she started a trend, opening doors for less famous stars to give their children ridiculous names.

See, Gwyneth Paltrow, as an A-lister, can get away with nonsense like that. Ashlee Simpson, who is C-list at best, can't. She named her son Bronx Mowgli Wentz, as if he weren't already saddled with enough baggage just by virtue of being the son of the Fall Out Boy and "the Simpson who isn't Jessica." According to the *San Francisco Chronicle*:

"[Pete] Wentz reveals Mowgli was inspired by the lead character in Rudyard Kipling's classic story, but he's refusing to reveal why they chose Bronx, also the name of one of New York's five boroughs. Wentz says, '*The Jungle Book* was something that me and Ashlee bonded over. It's a cool name.' "

Maybe they saw it on a highway sign or on a list of "The Top Ten Places Not to Go." Or maybe when their baby was born, they realized their child was about to be raised by fun-loving, if unprepared, jungle creatures. (Except those movie animals could sing.) I'm not actually convinced they had a reason at all.

Nicole Richie and Joel Madden, who gave their firstborn, Harlow Winter Kate, a decent enough name, really went for the full trash can when they chose Sparrow James Midnight Madden for their second child. What a lesson in superfluous middle names, especially since they don't compensate for the garbage surrounding them. Sparrow? No, thank you. That is my second least favorite bird, after the common street pigeon. And Madden, if you haven't learned, means nothing in this town. Actually, I'm not sure if the guy in this photo is Joel Madden or a character from some preschool television show.

But fear not, little children! You can legally change your name when you turn eighteen, or younger if you have parental consent. (This is how, at fifteen, Destiny Hope Cyrus became Miley Cyrus. Destiny made better choices.) For some celebrity babies, the name change comes even earlier.

Meg Ryan, who I think used to be famous like forty years ago (maybe even before talkies), adopted a baby girl from China and named her Charlotte, only to realize later that her daughter was more of a Daisy—because moving from China and finding out your mom has already spent your college money on Botox isn't enough of an adjustment. Meg said she settled on *Daisy* because her baby "is a really ridiculously happy person, and it was the happiest name I could think of."

It didn't take long for David Boreanaz, D-lister, to regret naming his baby Bardot, after Brigitte, a sex symbol of yesteryear and a

known racist. It was a particularly uncomfortable choice once Boreanaz's, ahem, dalliances hit the press. (Other names for philanderers to avoid naming their legitimate children: *Monica, Camilla, Soon-Yi.*) Soon, the Boreanazes renamed their daughter Bella, because, you know, when you can't use actresses of classic film for inspiration, there's always *Twilight*.

The ultimate lesson here is that names matter, and just because you're a C-list celebrity now doesn't mean you're going to stay there, and it definitely doesn't mean you're going to move up. You better believe that Jason Lee's son is going to be really upset that his father, in a fit of B-list stupidity-slash-megalomania, named him Pilot Inspektor. Especially because you are probably Googling "Jason Lee" right now to make sure you're thinking of the right guy.

# CELEBRITY TWINS

**THE TWIN BIRTHRATE IN THE UNITED STATES IS ON THE**
rise, hovering around 33 twin births per 1,000 babies. But in the
celebrity community, where in vitro fertilization is easier to come
by than a good plastic surgeon, it feels as though there are twins
at every turn—and that scares me because I've had anxiety about
twins ever since I realized that Mary-Kate and Ashley Olsen are

two different people. Different, but
equally terrifying.

Of course, the most famous young
twins are Brad and Angelina's, Knox
and Vivienne. As if just one more
Jolie-Pitt wouldn't be considered a
fate worse than death for this beautiful bastion of celebrity decorum, the
universe had to provide two. Admittedly, the twins haven't been as much
of a headache as their older children,
but still.

Other twins include those born via surrogacy to Sarah
Jessica Parker, Neil Patrick Harris, and Céline Dion. FYI: the Harris
kids are friendly, the Parker-Brodericks are not, and I've never met
Céline's. (Later in this book, you'll understand why.)

The fact that Céline Dion, Jennifer Lopez, and Mariah Carey
all have twins is a frightening reality. I believe they were all trying
to out-baby each other, and if one of them had managed to have

triplets, they would've been unspeakably proud of themselves. It definitely would've sealed up the headlining act at *VH1 Divas*. Beyoncé must feel like such a failure.

Hollywood is also populated by lesser-known twins. Dolly and Charlie O'Connell, for instance, are the daughters (yep, both daughters) of Jerry O'Connell and Rebecca Romijn. (They'd be cuter if they were John Stamos's.)

Charlie Sheen and Brooke Mueller have twin sons together, Max and Bob. And Julia Roberts, whose children could be so much more famous than they are, has twins Phinneaus and Hazel. Who knows, maybe it isn't her reclusive lifestyle in New Mexico keeping those kids quiet. Maybe the name *Phinneaus* is really holding him back. Oh gosh, I'm distracted by that photo of Rebecca. There are two of them. And there are two of her. I'm so uncomfortable.

# CELEBRITIES WHO SHOULD HAVE BABIES

**I'M NOT EXACTLY LOOKING FOR COMPETITION, BUT**
it does get kind of boring around here with just Harper Beckham and Blue Ivy Carter to scheme against. (And, really, they're babies. It's not that hard.) So who are the celebrities I'd like to see shake things up around here and give me something better to work with?

## Jennifer Aniston

**JENNIFER ANISTON HAS REPEATEDLY TOLD THE PRESS**
that she is not looking to have her life validated by producing a child. "That doesn't measure the level of my happiness or my success in my life," she told Gayle King. Okay, Jen. We know. We get it. Your life is not defined by an Aniston baby. Neither is mine. But for the rest of America, nay, the rest of the *world*, life is meaningless without the offspring of Jennifer Aniston and the partner of her choosing.

Do you know how much easier

my life would be if she and Brad Pitt had had children together and never broken up? Shiloh Jolie-Pitt is probably tearing out the pages of this book and eating them as we speak. Jennifer Aniston's baby would be cool, cultured, and probably really fun at parties, and I think I could be happy giving her some West Coast territory—probably Venice, possibly Santa Monica, depending on the quality of her highlights. (This, of course, would be in exchange for loyalty and cash.)

Jennifer, we know that beneath your sun-kissed hair and perfectly toned arms is a heart that will not be healed until you provide the world with a child. The universe is willing to compromise and will even accept you having a baby with Justin Theroux at this point, even though he is obviously beneath you and probably a creep. Please, Jen. Stop making everyone sad and have a baby already.

### Jon Hamm and Jennifer Westfeldt

**YOU KNOW, I DON'T EVEN CARE** about Jennifer Westfeldt so much, but she is Jon Hamm's chosen companion, and thus Jon Hamm's children she must bear. I have no idea why there has yet to be a contract to this effect. Westfeldt has stated

publicly that they are considering having children in the future, but that it's "not for us just yet."

But can you imagine how beautiful those kids would be? Even if you have no idea who Jennifer Westfeldt is, you have to admit the children would be shockingly perfect. After all, Mr. Hamm is just Don Draper but without the angst. It wouldn't make a good television show, but the children will be better adjusted.

You have no idea how much it frustrates me that we can't manage to get Jon Hamm to have one child, while there are now nineteen people with Jim Bob and Michelle Duggar's DNA in their bodies. Whatever happened to survival of the fittest? The world needs more people who can wear skinny ties and properly host *Saturday Night Live*.

## Ryan Gosling and Rachel McAdams

**I AM NOT SURE WHO BROKE UP WITH** whom, but I am convinced that if that person had not done that tremendously stupid deed, there would be a McAdams-Gosling baby by now and the world would be a better place. I would even forego my right to be threatened by their baby. (And believe me, I would have that right.) Beautiful, serious, and carried down New York City streets by Ryan Thomas Gosling—*this* is the American dream.

The good news is, it's not too late! Dump your significant others and get back together already! I think you owe it to everyone, and especially to your future celebrity children. One day, mark my words, the world will see Ryan Gosling holding a tiny Canadian baby, and the world will thank me.

## Dame Helen Mirren

**THESE DAYS, YOU'RE NEVER TOO OLD,** and Dame Helen is just one of the loveliest, most sincere ladies in Hollywood. More than almost anyone, she should have a legacy. Do you think Kristin Cavallari needs to leave behind her DNA for the planet to benefit from? Neither do I, but she has a baby anyway.

## Leonardo DiCaprio and Kate Winslet

**DO YOU EVEN KNOW WHAT AMERICA WOULD DO IF A** Winslet-DiCaprio union ever actually happened? They would need to close the New York Stock Exchange just to be safe—that's how wild and unpredictable this country would become. But despite the fact that it could throw us into a temporary recession (because we would all be out in the streets on parade, naturally), this needs to happen. They are both finally single, they are both still enjoying incredible career success, and *Titanic* is now available in 3-D. The only thing that could make it more real is for this couple to break the fourth wall and admit they are in love with each other already.

Winslet admitted that while filming the *Titanic* scenes where the ship finally sinks, she and DiCaprio shared intimate private conversations:

"Leo and I just hung on to each other for dear life...and the two of us literally were having conversations like, 'What would happen if we died?' And I'd say things like, 'Leo, I love you, I really do love you so much. You are a very important person to me and I'd have your babies. I would, I'd have your babies.'"

So why haven't you already?

A potential Winslet-DiCaprio child would have a lot of things that I don't have: dual British-American citizenship, shared history with the greatest love story ever told, and parents with actual talent. But it almost seems like fate, like something even I shouldn't interfere with or plot against. And I wouldn't. In fact, look at me: I'm encouraging it.

Bring it on.

# WHO'S DOING IT RIGHT

**I HATE TO ADMIT IT, BUT I** can be the bigger person here and say that Jay-Z and Beyoncé are doing a really good job making Blue Ivy Carter famous. Here's their recipe for success with Baby Knowles-Z:

1. Announce pregnancy in the most aggressively ostentatious way possible. Beyoncé dropped her baby bombshell at the MTV Video Music Awards, telling the audience, "I want you to feel the love that's growing inside of me!" and then bursting into "Love on Top." After belting out the song, she threw the microphone to the floor, unbuttoned her blazer, and rubbed her baby bump in an announcement that, while technically silent, was still loud enough for me to hear it over the blood boiling in my ears.

2. Find balance between showy, cute, and extremely private. Beyoncé is an unstoppable machine of good PR. She maintained her and Blue's privacy throughout her pregnancy and delivery by doing things like renting out full floors of the hospital and vacationing on a private island. She didn't like to talk

openly about her pregnancy, but when she did, she said adorable-mom things like, "The best thing is knowing that my favorite person in the world—I haven't met them yet." Gag me.

3. Name baby something unique and controversial. It's a color! It's a plant! It's symbolic of Beyoncé's favorite number and Jay-Z's album series! It's also totally dumb.

4. Release pictures in a pretentious, but populist way. Jay-Z and Beyoncé released photos of Blue Ivy not through an image distributor or a magazine shoot, but on her own website: helloblueivycarter.tumblr.com. They released them to the world free, as if they were doing the world a mitzvah, stating, "We welcome you to share in our joy." As if Blue Ivy Carter is their gift to the world. Please. Did she come with a gift receipt?

Of course, no one did a celebrity birth announcement better than yours truly. The mystery, the subterfuge, the pure desperation for a glimpse of my face—it all paid off when Annie Liebowitz shot mountaintop portraits of me (and some other people) for the cover of *Vanity Fair*. To this day, my debut for the magazine is second only in newsstand sales to the issue with a post-Pitt interview with Jennifer Aniston. You're welcome, Graydon.

# PART 2

# Celebrity Dynasties: The Modern-Day Feudal System

*Our founding fathers decided to do away with aristocracy, but that doesn't mean there aren't families better than yours.*

**I**N HOLLYWOOD, CELEBRITIES DON'T CREATE families—they create dynasties. While some celebrity parents can produce a reliably fameworthy child on the first shot (hello!), it takes others a few more tries. The Afflecks are on their third, and they still haven't managed to produce a worthy heir. Some celebrities have chosen to reproduce with commoners. Julia Roberts's children are basically nobodies, despite their half-pedigree, because the most promising celebrity babies are those born to not one, but two A-listers.

While Blue Ivy Carter is certainly a threat on her own, the real trouble won't come until Beyoncé and Jay-Z start populating Manhattan with a whole island full of attention-stealers.

## The Smiths

**THE SMITHS WILL NOT SLEEP UNTIL THEIR DAUGHTER,** my intolerable frenemy, Willow, is more famous than Katy Perry. This is probably not going to happen. They have invested millions trying to make Jaden Smith the male Dakota Fanning—also a fool's errand. (Dakota dresses better, and she knows how to throw a decent brunch.)

Shakespeare tells us, "Some are born great, some achieve greatness, and some have greatness thrust upon them." Try as they may, the Smiths will never succeed at thrusting greatness or talent upon their children, and all you need is one slumber party at Willow's house to know that she is not that special. They *have* built a rather large practice stage and a rather large (as yet uncomfortably empty) shrine for all of the awards they expect Willow to win, though.

This makes for awkward dinner parties with the Smith family, because they are oblivious to their own mediocrity. (Also because they are in desperate need of a remedial lesson in din-

ner utensils.) But seriously, we are close personal friends and I love them to pieces.

The world cringed when Willow, then ten years old, had the audacity to call Oprah Winfrey "girl" on her own show. There are three people in the world who deserve to be called "ma'am" under all circumstances: the Queen, Meryl Streep, and Oprah. And despite a handful of hit singles and even more dreadful hairstyles, Willow still has not lived that down in our circles. She hasn't gotten the full blacklist treatment, obviously, but let's just say that Willow has had a hard time getting dinner reservations in Chicago since then.

Meanwhile, Mr. and Mrs. Smith seem to be constantly swarmed by divorce rumors. I myself believe that they stay together because Willow is just too much work for one person. (She once tried to set my hair on fire.) Trey and Jaden are much lower-maintenance, which I think their parents see as a sign of weakness.

I'd like to say their moment is coming to an end, but you never know how much money these people will spend clinging to their relevance or the dream that their daughter will be a hair-whipping superstar. Oh, and by the way? The photo of them on page 25— dressed to impress and taking themselves super-seriously—was taken at the premiere of Justin Bieber's biopic *Never Say Never*.

## The Afflecks

IF YOU WANT TO KNOW ABOUT CAMPING, SHOPPING AT
Goodwill, or feeding a family on a budget, the Afflecks are the
ones to ask. Although I assume the Afflecks are doing all right,
they dress their three children as if they are one bounced check
away from the poorhouse. (And don't get me started on Jennifer
Garner's everyday wardrobe—she gave up on herself some-
where around 2006.)

The Affleck girls frustrate me because they have so much
potential. Seraphina is perhaps the second most beautiful child
in Hollywood, and Violet has a uniquely expressive face. If they
would just give up their folksy, lemonade-stand-for-the-
paparazzi act, they could be a competitive force in the celebrity-
child market.

The family stays in the news by being quote-unquote "normal."
(Why anyone would want this reputation, I have no idea.) Perhaps average, real-American housewives feel they can relate to

Jennifer Garner, with her oversized sweatpants, oafish husband, and under-achieving daughters. While she may like being known as Hollywood's Soccer Mom, I continue to implore (by polite, handwritten notes, as well as public shaming) Mrs. Affleck to *at least* hire someone to wash her hair every day. Because while Violet and Seraphina certainly look like two of the happiest children in Hollywood, they really should be ashamed of themselves.

Thank goodness their latest is a boy. Maybe little Samuel will avoid repeat-ing his sisters' mistakes. Oh, who am I kidding? Let's just hope he's funny.

## The Beckhams (*Swoon*)

**THE BECKHAM FAMILY, HEADED BY FOOTBALL/SOCCER/**
whatever star David Beckham and Victoria "Posh" Beckham, can
really do no wrong in my eyes. Already American royalty, it's only
a matter of time before the Queen knights David Beckham and
gives this family official titles in their home country.

*[Note to self: look up courtesy titles and related rights of
daughters-in-law upon marriage.]*

The Beckhams have a knack for timing their babies to low
points in their careers, making sure each child comes at an
opportune time to reassert their fame and dynastic power.
Never was this executed with more skill and savvy than with the
2011 arrival of Harper Seven Beckham. After eleven years rais-
ing sons (Brooklyn, Romeo, and the oh-so-debonair Cruz), Victoria Beckham finally managed to produce a daughter.

While people in other parts of the world prefer sons, Hollywood is ruled by daughters. The clothes, the attitudes, the

clothes ... having a baby girl is hitting the jackpot in the celebrity community. (Well, unless that girl turns out to be Shiloh Jolie-Pitt, but more on that later.) Arriving on the heels of three older brothers—and to a family desperately in need of a baby clotheshorse, a clothespony if you will—Harper was a welcome addition to our little circle of friends.

See, I've been close with the Beckhams for years, because I like English people, beautiful people, and people who have money. And Cruz and I have had a marriage contract almost since

birth, which I intend to enforce—his "feelings contract" will never hold up in court. It sounds old-fashioned, but I'm getting the better end of this bargain.

*[Note to self: look up British citizenship-upon-marriage laws.]*

# The Robertses (Nobodies)

**AFTER DATING A SERIES OF FAMOUS MEN, INCLUDING**
Dylan McDermott and Benjamin Bratt, Julia Roberts married a
cameraman and moved to Taos, New Mexico, which might as well
be Siberia. I think she lives in a pre-Columbian pueblo dwelling.
There are cave paintings and everything.

They have three children: Finn, Hazel, and Henry, each one
blonder and paler than the last. And now she lives the life of a
recluse, coming out of the desert for the occasional film and
press junket. That life seems to suit her, I suppose, after spend-
ing the nineties as America's Sweetheart. But living that far from
civilization and attention is not doing her children any favors in
terms of garnering affection from the paparazzi or the American
public.

Doesn't she know that if she wants to raise the *next* generation
of America's sweethearts she has to properly train them—and
get that Hazel some decent highlights and a spray tan? And for
that, you really have to stick to the coasts, plus the occasional
exotic filming location. Julia keeps busy these days with about
one movie a year, which is going to render her irrelevant before
she knows it. And *then* where will her children be?

## The Kardashians (Ugh)

**I WOULDN'T EVEN INCLUDE THEM HERE, EXCEPT THAT**
even the oldest money has to admit that these people are in the
zeitgeist, no matter how shallow and gross they are. They
became famous because their dynasty came ready-made—there
are already so *many of them.*

Mason Disick, son of Kourtney Kardashian and her ne'er-do-well
boyfriend/occasional fiancé, is the only true child of the bunch,
although there are teen daughters and, of course, Khloé. The Kardashian machine is trying very hard to make Mason a famous
celebrity baby, putting him in designer clothes and dragging him to
loads of events. And when it comes to Mason deserving such
attention—well, let's just say he makes Willow Smith look like
Dame Maggie Smith.

When you think about it, though, Mason is really the only Kardashian with any sort of potential. He's smart enough to have already realized that his family is so dull, even an imaginary friend is improvement upon them. At age two, he already had an imaginary friend named Donna. Life is so rough in that house, and those people are so vapid, that the two-year-old had to invent more interesting people to hang out with. And honestly, I bet that empty air is more cultured than any real person in that child's life.

It makes me happy to know that one day the Kardashians will be irrelevant. I cannot wait for the time when we get an annual update on these losers, chronicling their descent into poverty and madness after squandering their millions on spray tans and facelifts. Mason will have to go to public school. They'll all have to get *jobs*. It's going to be awesome.

## The Klum-Seals

**HEIDI AND SEAL HAD IT ALL: BEAUTY, FAME, CHILDREN**
with the most perfect multi-ethnic skin color you've ever seen,
and a really great Hollywood love story. Heidi Klum and Seal
started dating while she was pregnant with her daughter Leni,
whose biological father is Italian racecar mogul and former fugi-
tive Flavio Briatore. Despite the circumstances, Seal embraced
Heidi and Leni; he was present at the baby's birth and eventually

adopted her. Heidi and Seal went on to have three more children: sons Henry Gunther Ademola Dashtu and Johan Riley Fyodor Taiwol, and daughter Lou Sulola. After marrying in 2005, Heidi and Seal renewed their vows every year on their anniversary, threw extravagant Halloween parties, and generally made the world believe in love again.

Then in January 2012, they called it quits, very publicly. And while I think everyone believes that the Klum-Seal children will be all right, what we're really concerned about is whether the world can weather this divorce. I mean, for the longest time, I believed that we celebrated Valentine's Day because it was the day Seal proposed to Heidi. And now, with only Tom Hanks and Rita Wilson, William H. Macy and Felicity Huffman, and Tom Cruise and Katie Holmes (okay, fine, Mother, I put it in the book, are you happy?) maintaining the illusion that true love can exist in Hollywood, I don't know what we're going to do.

## The Richards-Sheens

**NOW HERE'S A WEIRD ONE. CHARLIE SHEEN AND DENISE** Richards are actually better together now than they ever were when they were married. Their daughters, the nuttily named Sam and Lola Sheen, are pretty average for Hollywood. They play soccer and are Girl Scouts, which are not exactly glamorous activities, unless you make enough money selling cookies to shop at Saks. Despite the messy divorce, the former family Sheen vacations together, now including Denise's adopted baby

daughter, Eloise. It's all very sweet and modern until you remember that Charlie Sheen, known crazy, has children, and Ryan Gosling does not.

## The Parker-Brodericks

**SARAH JESSICA PARKER AND MATTHEW BRODERICK** live a very New York lifestyle. They walk their children to school, they make time for Broadway shows, and I believe they maintain secret separate apartments. (Just a theory.) Together they have three children: son James Wilkie and twin daughters Tabitha and Loretta. It's very hard to picture SJP as a warm mother, and she certainly doesn't come across that way in interviews or in the critically reviled *I Don't Know How She Does It*. (I didn't see that movie, as I refuse to support the career of Olivia Munn. She knows what she did.) But this family is interesting because they seem to have stepped right out of Sondheim's *Company* or a Woody Allen movie, or basically anything that involves functional weirdness, narcissism, and affectionless marriages.

## The Jolie-Pitts

**WHEREAS I HAVE MADE A NAME FOR MYSELF BY BEING**
fastidiously groomed and extraordinarily well behaved at all
times, the Jolie-Pitts are famous for being the exact opposite.
Their parents allow the children to express themselves at any
expense. This may be liberating for the six of them, but it's insuf-
ferable to the rest of the world.

**Name:** Maddox Chivan Jolie-Pitt
**Birthday:** August 5, 2001
**Adopted:** March 10, 2002
**Country of Origin:** Cambodia
**Distinctive Attributes:** Maddox sports an occasional Mohawk hairstyle, prefers military chic garb, and has an affinity for hats. As the oldest of the Jolie-Pitts, he usually stays above the riffraff of the younger children.

**Name:** Zahara Marley Jolie-Pitt
**Birthday:** January 8, 2005
**Adopted:** July 6, 2005
**Country of Origin:** Ethiopia
**Distinctive Attributes:** Scowling. Zahara often appears tired by the antics of her siblings (namely Shiloh), making her the most serious Jolie-Pitt and thereby my favorite. Believe me, that is not as high a compliment as it may sound.

**Name:** Shiloh Nouvel Jolie-Pitt
**Birthday:** May 27, 2006
**Country of Origin:** Namibia (born there to pretentious American parents)
**Price of First Magazine Pictures:** $7.6 million—and was she *worth it?*
**Distinctive Attributes:** Messy hair and menswear are Shiloh Jolie-Pitt's most well-known features. (It's sad, but it's true.)

**Name:** Pax Thien Jolie-Pitt
**Birthday:** November 29, 2003
**Adopted:** March 15, 2007
**Country of Origin:** Vietnam
**Price of First Magazine Pictures:** $2 million +
**Distinctive Attributes:** Who even knows? Pax is the most mysterious of the Jolie-Pitts,' and very little is known about his character. He seems to be more camera-shy than the others and rarely does anything to provoke attention. In any other family, his enigmatic nature might make him more of a commodity. Call it

"The Louis Bullock Factor." But here, surrounded by crazies, being quiet just makes him the sixth Jolie-Pitt.

*Name:* Knox Léon and Vivienne Marcheline Jolie-Pitt

*Birthday:* July 12, 2008

*Country of Origin:* France (again, born abroad to Americans disappointed with non-exotic children)

*Price of First Magazine Pictures:* $14 million

*Distinctive Attributes:* Well, they are twins. Knox is almost indistinguishable from big sister Shiloh at this point, and I am not entirely sure what unique qualities, if any, he brings to the table. Vivienne, meanwhile, is shaping up to be the most fashionable of the Jolie-Pitts. Unlike those of her siblings, her clothes usually fit, and she occasionally brings out a truly lovely outfit. Oh, also, Brad Pitt once fell over while carrying her and tore his Achilles' tendon, so she could stand to lose a few.

# WHO'S DOING IT RIGHT

**THE BECKHAMS, OBVIOUSLY,** although they should quit while they're ahead. It'd be hard to improve upon the success of Harper Beckham, and despite their claims that they want more children, another Beckham baby might just jump the shark.

**THE ALBA-WARRENS** have two beautiful, charismatic daughters already (Honor and Haven) and could potentially raise a whole pack of camera-friendly children. The challenge for them is that they are just not famous enough. Jessica Alba's husband is a no-name, and unless the tide really turns, she's never going to be an A-lister, despite how deserving her daughters may be of a higher title.

**ME, OF COURSE.** I successfully lobbied my parents to stop at one. When you manage perfection on the first try, there's really no need to keep going. (Also, I need every resource of the Holmes-Cruise empire at my personal disposal, so another sibling just isn't in the cards.)

# PART 3

# Dressed to Distress: Celebrity Child Fashion

*I wish Grace Kelly, Princess Diana, and Jackie O were still alive. Then we could spend this whole chapter talking about them and their fashion contributions to the world. But they're not, and their young modern equivalents are like a waking nightmare.*

# Ava Phillippe: The Friendly Hipster

**AVA IS ABLE TO PULL OFF EVEN** the most casual of ensembles because of a unique talent for accessorizing and incorporating bold colors. In this photo, Ava matches a super-boring shorts/hoodie combination with fun eyeglasses, a sassy pose, and not one but *two* bags. She even gets away with more masculine pieces, like those sneakers, because she's otherwise very cute and girly. I've seen her wear witch boots with a vintage yellow sundress and thought she pulled it off. Although her style isn't really my style— meaning she wears pants and flats—I completely approve.

# Violet Affleck: The Granny

**EVERY ONCE IN A WHILE,** Violet Affleck pulls out a cute, trendy dress, and for a moment, I feel so happy. I've been trying to be her fashion mentor for *years*, and I feel a twinge of pride whenever she wears something remotely appropriate. Unfortunately, those moments are few and far between, and are usually accompanied by utter disappointment when I notice her accessories. Take this outfit, for example. The dress is cute enough—and it better be, because it will undoubtedly be passed down to younger sister Seraphina next—but she pairs it with what appear to be orthopedic sandals, a

backpack, and her frumpy father, who hasn't looked clean since *Pearl Harbor*. (On the bright side, at least the backpack is kind of fun?)

Get it together, Violet. It can be fun to mix designer labels with more affordable, Target-chic pieces—but it's even more fun not to.

# Harper Beckham: The Brit

**PEOPLE WANT TO** believe that Harper Beckham and I are going to be rivals. This could not be further from the truth. I have no quarrel with well-dressed, well-mannered young celebrities—it's the slovenly little miscreants I take offense at. (And if you think I'm going to be jealous of a baby's wardrobe, let me just remind you that I have invested $100,000 of Tom's money in my shoe collection.)

However, there are a lot of things that Harper Beckham has that I don't: a family connection to the royals, a permanent invitation to New York Fashion Week, and dual British/American citizenship. What I do have, however, is a figure. In the oohing and aahing over her admittedly cute face, everyone seems to overlook that Harper has a rather shapeless body, forcing her mother to dress her in shift dress after shift dress. Were it not for her trendy headbands or expensive tights, people would be forced to focus on how lumpy Harper Beckham is. (And really, she is.) Also, her hair is kind of thin.

What I'm trying to say is that Harper Beckham's style isn't as groundbreaking as the press would have you believe. For heaven's sake, she doesn't even wear *shoes*. Shoes!

# Louis Bullock: The Dapper Gent

**WHAT MAKES LOUIS BULLOCK (PRONOUNCED "LOO-EE,"** not "Loo-iss"—it's a common mistake) such a distinguished chap isn't just his penchant for scarves and hats, but the standard to which he holds himself. From the first photo we all saw of him, being held aloft in his mother's hands on the cover of *People*, Louis has been the most serious baby in Hollywood, a stoic, cultured, somewhat scowly young gentleman who seems straight off the pages of a Victorian

novel. Louis Bullock is like the Mr. Rochester of my generation, only instead of an insane wife, his attic is filled with Warhol prints and last-season newsboy caps.

He can get away with wearing jeans to school, because his expression always conveys that he is not to be trifled with. (I could wear jeans if I wanted to, but *ick*.) He frequently wears tiny newsboy caps, tiny aviator hats, and a wide assortment of jackets, but it's his expression that makes his debonair style famous. You know what they say: you're never fully dressed without a frown.

# Mason Disick: The Poser

**THE THING ABOUT MASON DISICK IS, HE JUST TRIES WAY** too hard. Every look his mother puts him in always seems just a tad *too* polished—and we all know Mason isn't capable of carrying off perfection on his own. Kourtney Kardashian tries so hard to make Mason a standout amongst celebrity babies, but he just

doesn't seem to care quite as much as his mother does. He always seems to be squinting or scowling—but not in a handsome, brooding Louis Bullock kind of way—and just generally not putting any personality behind his outfits. It's okay, some people just aren't cut out for the stress of being a celebrity child, and boys definitely seem more recalcitrant. It's just sad because Kourtney so desperately wants him to play the part. Better luck with Baby #2, KK.

But just know, as long as your children are part of the Kardashian family, they will never truly fit into the exclusive world of high-fashion child couture. If there's one thing you should have learned from your reality television predecessors, it's that money can't buy you class.

## Ava Jackman: The Carefree Clasher

**AVA JACKMAN, DAUGHTER OF HUGH JACKMAN, HAS** taught me many things, such as: What a "scooter" is; what a "hoodie" is; that her mother, Deborra-Lee Furness, is not Olivia Newton-John's older sister.

What I have *not* learned from Ava Jackman is anything about style. To her credit, Ava can be fearless about fashion. Unfortunately, rather than risky endeavors with high-class payoff, this child's choices more often end in sartorial disaster. Her style can best be described as "urban boring," and she frequently wears—in one outfit—more brown articles of clothing than I have in my entire wardrobe. The outfit pictured here involves drawstring shorts over what can only be described as pajama pants, a yellow zip-up jacket that matches nothing, and shoes with laces. She's also ready to go with that ridiculous scooter, her favorite mode of transportation. You know what my favorite mode of city transportation is? A car service.

## Coco Arquette: The Pantsless Princess

**SO MANY WONDERFUL** celebrity experiences are wasted on Coco Arquette: front row at New York Fashion Week, sitting with Cher at *Dancing with the Stars*, and, really, having her picture taken at all. Coco's parents clearly overindulge her, particularly after their uncomfortably public separation and divorce, but it's gone far enough now. Coco is frequently photographed going outside in very short dresses, or in tights with not-quite-long-enough shirts. I just wish she would take herself a little more seriously than bad highlights and basically wearing underpants in public. Considering her lineage, I suppose it's not entirely unexpected, but it's still disappointing.

## Willow Smith: The Drunken Muppet

**WILLOW SMITH *THINKS* SHE IS THE LADY GAGA OF THE** celebrity-child red carpet with her daring, innovative, shock-and-awe-type fashion. But in reality, Willow Smith is the Nicki Minaj of the celebrity-child red carpet: annoying. Her "style" is all but nonexistent; rather, she wears clothes that are far off-trend, uninspired, and often just plain crazy. I mean, what was she going for with this nasty-brown pants and glitter skirt combination? Did she come to the Kids' Choice Awards as a space chef with her apron on backward? Is that little bag where she plans to keep her tips? Well, here's the only tip you're going to get, Willow: you're trying too hard and it's making my eyes tired.

# Flynn Bloom: The Distracter

**FLYNN BLOOM, SON OF ORLANDO BLOOM AND HIS MODEL** wife Miranda Kerr, is one of those babies who has struggled with his hairline as evidenced by the hood his mother puts on his head. It's disappointing, because his father's hair is better than just about everything else Orlando has going for him, including

his acting abilities. The good news for Flynn is that he has a few more years to try and get something started up there. With any luck, he won't end up with the full Prince William.

Miranda loves to dress Flynn in horizontal stripes, and, frankly, he looks a little too much like the boy from *The Addams Family* for that to be a good idea. Honestly, for the child of a supermodel, his fashion isn't much to speak of, but you can tell that this child's personality is going to take him where he needs to go. I mean, look at that face—it's almost enough to distract you from the fact that he's wearing shoes that Velcro.

Boys have everything so easy.

# Nahla Aubry: The Hair

**MEANWHILE, HALLE BERRY'S DAUGHTER, NAHLA, HAS**
possibly the fourth best hair in the world. (You know, after yours truly, Taylor Swift, and Kate Middleton.) It's very season-one-*Felicity*, actually. That girl wears some of the most uninspired chil-dren's clothes in all of California, but she gets away with it because her hair is so beautiful. Are you even noticing the fact that she is wearing five different clashing colors in this photo? In addition to the outrage I feel at this black skirt/brown boots combi-nation, I shudder to imagine what the thread count on that shirt is. And those boots look as though they were stolen off one of Snow White's dwarfs or an anima-tronic child inside It's a Small World. It's lazy, and it *reeks* of organized pre-school, an experience I masterfully avoided.

# Shiloh Jolie-Pitt: The Failure

**ANGELINA CALLS SHILOH'S** look "Montenegro style." I'm not sure what she was suggesting, but that is now my favorite insult to anyone's lack of fashion sense. (Katie Holmes? Serious Montenegro style.) Shiloh is a fan of graphic tees, hand-me-downs, cargo pants, and, above all, menswear. I have no real problem with Shiloh preferring menswear—even I can admit that it has become her style trademark, and I approve of individuality to a certain extent. What I have a problem with is Shiloh consistently choosing ill-fitting, often stained menswear. Her closet must look so much like a war zone that pretty soon her mother's going to want to adopt children from there.

# Kingston Rossdale: The Renegade

**IN WHAT UNIVERSE IS THIS** fur-vest-cape-jacket okay? Not only is it gross, but it's also about as fashion-backward as one can get. Did he get this from the *Game of Thrones* rejected-costumes dumpster? Kingston Rossdale is always wearing some crazy concoction of pieces, as if the whiter he dyes his hair, the crazier it makes his brain. And you know what? Most of the time, he gets away with it, that son of a gun. I've seen Kingston Rossdale wearing short-shorts, high-tops, and a lavender tank top, and the ladies at the party were still fawning over him. I don't get it.

Also, graphic tees belong on the sale rack at Walmart and never on the backs of the wealthy.

## Honor Warren: The Classy Bohemian

**LET'S PUT IT THIS WAY: HONOR WARREN IS WEARING** cut-off jean shorts in this picture, and yet she is somehow making it work. The trendy half-sweater, the pink sandproof tights, the where-did-you-get-those ankle riding boots—it's an outfit that says

"I own a lot of clothes," but also, "And you can totally borrow them anytime, because I'm NICE." (My outfits have never said anything like that.) I'd be threatened by Honor's approachable, everygirl style were it not for the fact that her parents are B-listers, at best, and her station is embarrassingly beneath mine. Still, it's good to feel a little competition from the lower classes to keep the rest of us on our toes. And she definitely has my toes on edge, because I'd never get my feet that close to public sand, even with shoes on. She's fearless, and that scares me. Today it's jorts in a sandbox; tomorrow, it could be overalls and cigarettes. Congratulations, Honor Warren. In the world of celebrity-child fashion, you are the 99 percent.

# Sasha Obama: The New Jackie

**SASHA OBAMA IS BEAUTIFUL, POISED, AND POWERFUL.**
Too bad her house is so much smaller than mine.

Here she is at a White House event, wearing a classy-casual power suit, made more youthful and fun by the addition of a funky, oversized brooch. I wish I had formal-fancy Washington events to attend: press briefings, Senate confirmation hearings, Watergate parking garage informant meetings. (I assume that as First Daughter, Sasha gets to do all of those things.) Sasha has already achieved what many older women struggle with—making professional outfits fresh. I find her style so inspiring, it makes me proud to be an American.

## Skylar Berman: Le Petit Fleur

**RACHEL ZOE'S BABY IS** impeccably well dressed, but he has what is probably the least masculine wardrobe in the industry. His mother is a fashion expert, and you get the idea that she was incredibly disappointed to give birth to a child of the male variety. So she decided to embrace men's runway fashion for her baby, putting him in all sorts of outrageous outfits that somehow always end up making Skylar Berman look like a tiny French sailor. Baby capelets, baby scarves, baby chapeaux— Rachel's not putting him in dresses or anything, but she's certainly not helping him earn any man points, either. It's only a matter of time before Rachel enters them in a creepy mother-son beauty pageant. It doesn't help that her baby has the bluest eyes and the longest lashes and the rosiest cheeks in the Western Hemisphere. He looks like a little porcelain doll come to life—and one who's arrived ready for his Latisse commercial.

## Suri Cruise: The Icon

**I WOULD DESCRIBE MY** style as twenty-first-century Audrey Hepburn, except that I use *all of* the colors. And I have better skin. Give me a pair of heels, a frilly dress, and a classic Burberry trench, and I'll out-outfit every girl in the industry. Now, I'd like to use this space to clear up a few misconceptions about my style and my mother's involvement in it.

*1.* Much has been made of my penchant for high heels. I wear them primarily because that's what ladies *do*, and I'm nothing if not a lady. But they have secondary benefits as well, such as improving my already-impeccable posture and making my father seem even shorter than he already is.

2. No one should criticize members of my family for my choice to go coatless in winter. Coats, my friends, are for quitters, and people who aren't proud of the clothes they're wearing underneath. I don't put a Givenchy sample size on so that the paparazzi can take pictures of my overcoat, do I?

3. I've been criticized for carrying expensive handbags at such a young age. But what do you expect me to do? Put my American Express black card in my pocket? Most of my dresses don't even *have* pockets!

4. I do occasionally wear lipstick. Tom calls it "a lady's prerogative."

# SURI'S BEST
# FASHION ADVICE

1. Always wear shoes. Going barefoot is how you get SARS.

2. Sleeveless tees have no place in modern society. Ditto graphic tees. The only time these are ever appropriate is when you are painting your house, so if you're wealthy, this means never.

3. The only people who should be wearing peasant tops are actual peasants. You know, like Seraphina Affleck.

4. One of life's greatest tragedies is that we are not born knowing how to dress ourselves. My mother dressed me in jeans once. JEANS. If your mother dresses you in sneakers and a shape-less, possibly homemade dress, the only thing you can do is smile.

5. Ladies do not paint their nails more than one color.

6. Take the no-white-after-Labor Day rule seriously. White win-terwear is a fashion oxymoron.

7. Almost everyone is rich enough to afford pants without holes.

8. Alicia Keys once said her baby son had the "cutest, most adorable sneakers." That is like saying there's a "prettiest

Kardashian." It's an impossibility. Shoes shouldn't have laces, Velcro, or lights.

9. Every outfit is an opportunity. Try harder than Crocs.

10. When clothes are "off the rack," that means they can give you body lice.

11. It's tacky to be seen in the same outfit twice, so once I've worn something, I have Katie send my dresses to less fortunate children, like Denise Richards's kids.

12. Cute, clever, and symmetrical: these are my rules for haircuts and for life in general.

13. *No one*, least of all Beyoncé, owns the color Blue.

# WHO'S DOING IT RIGHT

**UM, CAN YOU READ?**

# PART 4

# Old Hollywood Money and the Nouveau Riche: Social Capital in the Modern Economy

*My money is extremely old.
Like,* Top Gun *old.*

SOCIETY USED TO HAVE BETTER WAYS OF MEASURING a person's value. You were either old money or new money, and you stuck to your kind. But nowadays, thanks to reality television and a rather gross music industry, it seems as though everyone has money. I still like to measure people according to the old standard, and let's just say, some of these families are paying their mortgage with money right off the printing press.

## Ava and Deacon Phillippe: Old Money

*Money comes from:* Quality films like *Walk the Line*, lower-quality films like *This Means War*, and child support payments from Ryan Phillippe

*Net worth:* $80 million

**ONE OF THE FEW CELEBRITY** births I've ever looked forward to is Reese Witherspoon's new baby. The only thing lovelier than Reese Witherspoon's two children is the likelihood that she might have even lovelier children with her handsome nobody of a husband, Jim Witherspoon. I assume he took her name when they got married, because, well,

who wouldn't? (When Cruz Beckham and I get married, his name is going to be Cruz Cruise—it's in the contract.)

The Witherspoons are an old-money family because of the way they behave: they go to church, they dress nicely, and they always have a smile on their face, even after their matriarch has been hit by a car. Deacon is the cleanest boy in Hollywood, after the Beckhams, and he dresses very sharply. Even his casual clothes are well fitted, and as you can see, he can already fill out a suit quite nicely, like a young, modern-day Don Draper. Except that you also get the idea that he respects women.

Ava, with her smiley-hipster style, is very much a Hollywood tween girl-next-door, and for once I don't mean that as an insult. Don't take this as an endorsement of hipster style, but rather of Ava Phillippe. She's cute and clever, while still being tasteful—the perfect combination of modernity and old-money class. If this family lived at Downton Abbey, she would be the Lady Sybil.

Reese married Hollywood agent Jim Toth in 2011, and they have since started their own family. I view this as the Witherspoons fulfill-

ing their responsibility to the industry to contribute counteragents to children like Mason Disick. You know, like how the baby boom was just the USA's plan to make sure the Russians didn't outnumber us.

# Sean Preston and Jayden Federline: New Money

**Money comes from:** Pop music, the tears of more deserving musicians

**Net worth:** $160 million

**NOTHING IN THE WORLD** makes me quite as sad as the fact that Britney Spears has money. If "Baby, One More Time" hadn't been successful, the entire Spears family would be back in Louisiana, eating crawfish with their fingers, wearing overalls, and singing Carrie Underwood karaoke, or whatever people in the South do when they don't have jobs.

Her sons are handsome enough, but I fear their gene pool may hold them back. They seem content with the life they have, which involves trampolines, above-ground pools, and seeing their mom in leotards. If there was any doubt that Britney and Kevin Federline had decided to raise the children redneck, there isn't any more. Look at Britney in this photo: she's wearing *flip-flops* to the theater. (I believe she and the children were invited to play the hyenas in this production of *The Lion King*.)

Also note that the Spears-Federline children are part of a package deal, as they come with their cousin, Maddie Briann Aldridge, the daughter of Britney's younger sister, Jamie Lynn. There aren't a whole lot of barbs to be made at Jamie Lynn's expense that haven't already been made, except to say that you would think teenagers—or any former Nickelodeon star, really—would be able to dress their child better. As it stands, it looks like everyone in the Spears family buys off-the-rack at Walmart or any of the other Marts, and usually not in their correct size.

There could be hope for them, if they'd immediately transfer to a boarding school and unlearn their mother's new-money ways. Until then, I will be maintaining a perimeter, because they seem like the kind of kids who enjoy scatological humor.

# Max and Emme Muñiz (A.K.A. the Lo-Anthony Twins): Old Money

**Money comes from:** Being the children of the most powerful Latinos in the world, after Selena's ghost and Fidel Castro

**Net worth:** $150 million

**OLD-MONEY FAMILIES** know the value of their children, and Jennifer Lopez has some of the oldest money in Hollywood. (*On the 6* came out in 1999, for crying out loud.) The children of old-money families exist to inherit their fortunes and, because their parents sometimes have reputations for being cold, to make them look friendly and normal. I am not sure if Jennifer Lopez's twins humanize her as much as she wishes they would, mostly because the twins are only ever seen at high-profile events, like *People* magazine covers or in her lap at *American Idol* or beside her in Gucci ads. Being old money means you can afford to be a little mysterious, but there's a balance. Why be a complete enigma when the attention is so *fun*?

I would love to know more about Max and Emme's personalities and styles. What inspires them? Where do they shop? What hair products do they use? I hope one day *they* write a book—from scratch, as ghostwritten books are very new money—sharing secrets of their family's inner circle.

## Naleigh Kelley: New Money

*Money comes from:* Bad movies and, I assume, some kind of deal with the devil

*Net worth:* $18 million

**NALEIGH KELLEY WAS ADOPTED FROM SOUTH KOREA BY** known shrew Katherine Heigl and her husband Josh Kelley. And, really, it's got to be disappointing to show up in America to find you're to be raised by the third most despised person in Hollywood, after Kate Gosselin and the Fox executive who canceled *Firefly*. But even Katherine Heigl's house (I call her by her full name because "Heigl" sounds too respectful, but "Katherine" too friendly) is better than a Korean orphanage, I suppose.

Katherine Heigl is committed to peddling her daughter around town and the talk shows, trying to make people believe that Naleigh is a fashion-forward toddler eyeing a film career. Listen

up, America: this is patently false. I ran into Naleigh at an event a few months back, and she complained about the kitten heels her mom made her wear. Old money would never complain about uncomfortable footwear.

I wish Naleigh the very best, I really do. She's in an impossible situation that will only change once she can be legally emancipated, or at least gets a stylist.

## Apple and Moses Martin: Old Money

*Money comes from:* A string of successful movies in the nineties, a string of bad movies in the oughts, and Coldplay

*Net worth:* $78 million, or as she would surely say, £48 million

**SAY WHAT YOU WILL ABOUT GWYNETH PALTROW—** goodness knows I have—but she comes from a solid Hollywood family, generally acts respectably, and doesn't outsource the fame-mongering to her children, which puts her firmly in the old-money camp. Sure, she surrounds herself with new-money types (cough, Jay-Z, cough) and puts on that fake British accent as if we don't know who she is, and she did that movie with Leighton Meester, but that's almost overlookable.

The Martins are a little removed from the Hollywood scene because they live most of the year in London. I am not sure if Apple and Moses are entirely aware of their standing in the celebrity community; it would certainly explain some of their outfits. If they really want to be relevant—like, as relevant as they were when they were born to a firestorm of incredulous press about their *names*—they're going to need to move back to California, or at least New York. I love England and plan to obtain dual citizenship upon my marriage to Cruz Beckham, but the attention just isn't the same, and unfortunately, Apple and Moses have fallen off the radar a little bit.

But then again so has Coldplay. And so has Gwyneth Paltrow's career.

# The Spelling-McDermotts: New Money

**Money comes from:** Reality television, plastic surgery prod-
uct placement

**Net worth:** A paltry $16 million

**THE WHOLE "REALITY**
show" thing should tip you
off to the fact that this family
is decidedly new money, but
this family also has a pet goat
that they walk down the street,
while also pushing the children
in a wheelbarrow—if that's not
irrefutable proof, then I don't
know what is. The only thing
worse than being a redneck
hillbilly is being a redneck
hillbilly on purpose to get
attention.

There are three children in
this family—Liam, Stella, and
Hattie—and they are all
blondes, which is strange because Tori's hair *can't* be genetically
accurate. They seem like relatively carefree little children, which

makes me sad because they clearly don't know just how rough it is over there. I mean, they keep a goat at their house. An actual goat.

The other thing that new-money families have a lot of is children. Tori and Dean have now brought a *fourth* child into this world. Old-money families like mine know better than to overproduce, but we sure are getting outnumbered by these people.

## Monroe and Moroccan Carey-Whatever: Old Money

*Money comes from:* Residuals from Mariah Carey's *nineteen* #1 singles, royalties from every single version of "All I Want for Christmas Is You," and whatever sad sum Nick Cannon contributes

*Net worth:* $525 million

### MONROE AND MOROCCAN CANNON—WHERE TO BEGIN?

Born into one of the oldest-money families in the celebrity

universe (Carey money is actually older than Nick Cannon himself), these twins have already met Barbara Walters, had an audience with Michelle Obama, and launched their own Internet startup, dembabies.com. Don't be fooled, though, they are still not the most important part of their family. Monroe and Moroccan were born to the sound of a recording of a live performance of Ms. Carey's "Fantasy," because she wanted them to hear the applause and know, from the very start, that they will be less important than she is until the day she dies.

As with other old-money families, there are few pictures of the Carey-Cannons out and about in public. You won't see them in *Us* magazine's "Stars: They're Just Like Us!" feature, because they are *not* just like you. It is as if these twins exist only when pulled out for appearances, like Spanx or a good pair of shoes.

## The Madonnas: New Money

*Money comes from:* Hits of the eighties and nineties

*Net worth:* $650 million

**YOU MIGHT THINK THAT MADONNA'S FAMILY WOULD**
be old money, just based on the fact that Madonna is old. But actually, she is one of the few celebrities who traded in her old money for new money. (The exchange rate is your dignity.)

Madonna has four children—five if you count her barely legal boyfriend, who is closer in age to her preliterate daughter than to Madonna herself. Her oldest daughter, Lourdes, is turning into quite the hot mess, too, doing such crazy things as shaving her head, dressing vaguely goth, and blogging without proofreading. Although looking at the photo on page 81, it's hard to blame her for leaping off the deep end. On the embarrassing scale, Madonna makes Katie look like the cool mom. And she wore overalls and Crocs to breakfast last week.

Despite having a huge dynasty and being one of the few best-

selling artists of the 1980s to still be, you know, alive, Madonna's class factor has been sorely affected by uncouth behavior and not aging gracefully. No one in the universe needed a new Madonna song featuring Nicki Minaj and M.I.A. When you have $650 million, you don't need to stay relevant. As for her children, they seem to go along with the act for the most part, but none of them remember the old-money days, either, which is probably a blessing and a curse.

# The Dion-Angélils: Old Money

**Money comes from:** Pop music, her Vegas show, and wherever vampires get cash

**Net worth:** $400 million

**CÉLINE DION MET HER** husband, René Angélil, when she was twelve and he was thirty-eight.

Although they did not start dating until later in their lives, most people contend that this is pretty darn creepy. (There's an age gap between my parents, as well, but not this pronounced. And let's be honest, Tom looks the same today as he did in *Risky Business*, a film he loves reenacting at parties.)

Their first son, René-Charles, was born in 2001. Almost ten years later, in 2010, Céline gave birth to twins, Nelson and Eddy. This is one of my favorite celebrity baby name stories. Eddy is named after Céline's favorite Algerian songwriter, Eddy Marnay, who is dead and

whom you have probably never heard of. And Nelson is named after former South African president and global champion of democracy, Nelson Mandela.

Clearly, Céline saw potential in at least one of her babies.

This family is old money not only because René Angélil is really, really old, but also because I am pretty sure they are vampires. I mean, their whole story reeks of *Twilight*—the debonair-ish older gentleman and the innocent young girl. Just look at René-Charles in that photo; if that's not a shifty-eyed vampire, then I don't know what is. It would explain why René is always wearing sunglasses inside and why they still spend so much time in Canada. (You know, because of the darkness.) Also, didn't Nelson Mandela do a lot of humanitarian work for the vampire cause in Eastern Europe? No?

Vampires are very wealthy because they have had such a long time to accrue interest, weather the market, and foresee long-term trends. Compound that with recording the theme song to *Titanic*, and you've hit the jackpot.

## The Ripa-Consueloses: New Money

*Money comes from:* Soap operas and daytime talk (my personal hell)

*Net Worth:* $55 million

### KELLY RIPA WON FIVE SOAP OPERA DIGEST AWARDS

for her role on *All My Children*, so you know she's a big deal. Ha.

The most notable new-money thing that Kelly and her husband Mark have ever done was during an appearance on *The Rachael Ray Show*. (Well, that is a new-money activity in and of itself, actually. The only daytime chat shows worth appearing on are Oprah's and Anderson Cooper's, and one of those isn't even on anymore.)

Anyway, while chitchatting with Rachael Whatever, they announced that they prefer their youngest son, Joaquin, to his siblings, Michael and Lola, even admitting that they would rescue Joaquin in a fire before the others. Listen, I've seen every Meryl Streep movie ever made, and *Sophie's Choice* is supposed to be harder than this.

They laughed and pretended like they were kidding, but I remain skeptical. The thing is, I can kind of understand it. Of the Ripa-Consuelos kids, Joaquin is the only one who has a firm handshake and doesn't order off the children's menu at nice restaurants. (That's very important to me. One of the most embarrassing moments in my life was watching Willow Smith try to order chicken fingers at Masa.) But things like this are unspoken in old-money families like mine—sure, we all know who'd get rescued first, but we certainly don't talk about it outside of the house or private security contracts.

## The McGraw Ladies: Old Money

*Money comes from:* Country music and that terrible Gwyneth Paltrow movie that I'll pretend never existed

*Net worth:* $77 million

**I AM NOT A FAN OF COUNTRY MUSIC, BUT YOU'D HAVE** to be dead inside not to be charmed by Tim McGraw and Faith

Hill's family. They have three daughters, Gracie, Maggie, and Audrey, and live in Nashville, so they aren't much of a bother to me. This family is an interesting breed of old money in that their money is southern. I think some of it is in Confederate quarters.

I am not really sure how the country industry works, but I assume that people like Taylor Swift and Miley Cyrus pop over to the McGraws for fritters and banjo picking on the regular. It's not really my style, but that could be a nice life, if you didn't mind living that far from a Bloomingdale's and a dependable sushi restaurant. And if you're going to live in a red state, you might as well do it in style.

The McGraws are the unchallenged rulers of country; in fact, I think they may have been elected Governors of Opryland or something. They're about as royal as you can get in the Deep South, and that makes their daughters the unofficial heiresses to Tennessee.

# Levi and Vida McConaughey: New Money

*Money comes from:* Movies, although I'd be hard-pressed to name a single one; that's how forgettable they are

*Net worth:* $65 million

**MATTHEW MCCONAUGHEY AND CAMILA ALVES HAVE**
two children together, Levi and Vida, and although the children

have beautiful faces, they are 50 percent redneck by birth and therefore difficult to take seriously. See, Mr. McConaughey is from Texas, and whereas the Southeast is all magnolias and yes, ma'ams, Texas is a desertlike plain of bad manners and big hair.

I mean, what do you even call the length of these cut-off jeans? Capri? And between the socks-with-sandals head-scratcher and the twisted-up suspender/binky combination, I'd be more likely to identify this child as homeless than as a member of the new-money elite. (Meanwhile, that stranger in a checkered coat is sullying the laws of fashion just by smiling at Levi. One must be ready to use a healthy scowl of disapproval when one is called for.)

The McConaugheys recently moved from Los Angeles to live permanently in Texas. That's a mistake. Do you think there's good shopping out on the prairie? I don't think they even have FedEx in the Lone Star State. All I had to do to decide I never wanted to go back to Texas was spend one layover at the Dallas airport and another afternoon at President Bush's ranch. Talk about boring.

## The Zeta-Jones-Douglases: Very Old Money

*Money comes from:* Modern classic films like *Chicago* and *The American President*

*Net worth:* $278 million

**NOT ONLY DOES MICHAEL DOUGLAS COME FROM A** distinguished Hollywood family, but he is also very, very old. He married Welsh actress Catherine Zeta-Jones or, as I like to call her, Cathy Jones, in 2000 when she was thirty-one and he was fifty-six. They have defied early skepticism and stayed married through his throat cancer, her bipolar diagnosis, and the birth of two children, Dylan and Carys. What makes the Zeta-Jones-Douglases so old money is that even the strangest celebrity business rolls right off their backs.

A twenty-five-year age difference? That's just how it's done.

Testifying against a stalker? Just another day at the office.

Michael Douglas's oldest son, Cameron, will be in prison until 2020. It happens.

Dylan and Carys have been raised very privately; the most public and old-money event that Carys has ever participated in was appearing at the 2003 Oscars in utero when Cathy won Best Supporting Actress for *Chicago*. Until 2010, the Douglases lived primarily in Bermuda; now, they reside in Manhattan. Bermuda is nice, because you can live like expats without having to actually leave the Western Hemisphere, but Manhattan is nicer. For starters, they don't have Broadway musicals every night in St. George's.

It's worth noting that this photograph was taken on the day Catherine Zeta-Jones was given the title of Commander of the Most Excellent Order of the British Empire (CBE) by Prince Charles. Fancy.

# The Hudson-Robinson-Bellamys: New Money

**Money comes from:** Lame romantic comedies and however her husbands make money

**Net worth:** $38 million

**LET'S JUST START BY SAYING** this: old money gets regular haircuts. Kate Hudson's oldest son, Ryder, used to have the longest, saddest hair in all of California.

Listen, I have no problem with children finding ways to express their personal style. What I have

a problem with is split ends and flat roots. And although Ryder now has a shorter, cropped hairstyle—basically the look I like to call "The Shiloh"—the memory of those long tresses lingers.

Since Ryder's birth in 2004, Kate has divorced her first husband and had a baby with Matthew Bellamy, lead singer of the band Muse, which I have never heard of but which I assume is lame. Her second son is named Bingham Hawn Bellamy (they call him "Bing"), and there are not enough eyerolls in the world to accurately describe how dumb I think that is.

Kate lives a kind of transient, flower-child lifestyle, which would be cute if she were poor. But when you have money, it's more appropriate to keep two or three homes (West Coast, East Coast, and preferably abroad) and put your children in exclusive private schools. Also, you should have better taste in husbands.

# THE CELEBRITY CHILDREN I'M OVER ALREADY

**ONE OF THE MOST NEW-MONEY THINGS A PERSON CAN** ever do is to wear out their welcome. This goes for dinner parties, vacations at a friend's beach villa, *and* being a celebrity. (Lady Gaga, I hope you are watching the clock.)

Here are the celebrity children I hope I never have to hear about ever again.

## Ella Travolta

**WILLOW SMITH, WATCH** and learn.

The Travoltas tried so hard to make Ella Bleu Travolta happen. They took her to red carpet events, they had her cast in John Travolta's film *Old Dogs* (currently at a 5 percent rating on Rotten Tomatoes), and they created an official website complete with a "fan space" that I occasionally spam when I get bored. Gems from this website include that her favorite actor is her dad, her favorite actress is her mom, and her favorite color is "rainbow." Wow. What a talent.

Anyway, her parents were completely intent on making her famous, and it pretty much backfired. Before her tenth birthday, Ella Travolta was already oversaturated in the market. Which actually worked out fine for just about everyone except her parents, who had invested so much money into her "career" that I'm sure they'll never forgive her for not trying hard enough.

It's okay, though. Her website says she has three more part-time jobs.

## Maxwell Drew Johnson

**I'VE BEEN OVER THIS BABY** since Halloween 2011, when Jessica Simpson decided to announce her pregnancy with a mummy costume. I've been over this baby since Jessica shared way too many details about her pregnancy and her marriage—things no human should ever have to hear. I've been over this baby since Jessica posed nude on the cover of *Elle* magazine, leaving me with an image that will be forever burned on my poor, undeserving eyes. I've been over this baby since before Jessica Simpson even met Eric Johnson. Actually, I still don't even know what that guy looks like.

It's too bad, really, that poor Maxwell—oh, right, she's a girl, by the way—was doomed before even being born. She didn't do anything wrong, other than being born to the world's most annoying narcissist since Barbara Walters.

## AND ANY OF THE FOLLOWING

children of C-list "celebrities":

1. Hilary Duff's baby

2. Kristin Cavallari's baby

3. Snooki's baby

4. The children of anyone who used to be on *Beverly Hills, 90210* but are now washed up

5. Selma Blair's baby

6. Any of the children born to the cast of *Grey's Anatomy*

7. Alicia Silverstone's baby, Bear Blu (come on now)

8. The Gosselins, the Duggars, and anyone else who made their money in reality television

9. Elisabeth Hasselbeck's children

10. Blue Ivy Carter

# HOW TO BE OLD MONEY

1. Embrace multiple names: Neiman Marcus, Bergdorf Goodman, Jacqueline Kennedy Onassis. Or embrace one-word names: Cher, Adele, Suri.

2. Ladies wear heels, because ladies do not hurry.

3. You are not a dock worker, a country singer, or a repressed nine-to-five office drone on Casual Friday. You do not wear jeans. (Ditto shoes with laces, graphic tees, and anything designed by Jessica Simpson.)

4. Your vacation spots should be reachable only by private plane. Do you think Richard Branson's private island has a commercial airport? Because it doesn't.

5. Learn the names of every character on *Downton Abbey*. Particularly the upstairs ones.

6. Keep lipstick handy at all times. Old money is never caught unawares.

7. Table etiquette is nothing to joke about. Bad dinner manners ruined Haley Joel Osment's career.

8. Don't carry cash, unless it is in British pounds, so you can tip a valet with class.

9. Never talk publicly about money, but

make sure your publicist leaks the price of your new real estate purchase to the press.

10. Surround yourself with famous friends. Stay away from anyone with the title "backup dancer."

11. Never be seen on the sidewalk, unless it is on the way from a lobby to a waiting car.

12. Public transportation is for the public—that means not you.

13. Don't be Katherine Heigl.

# WHO'S DOING IT RIGHT

**ARE YOU KIDDING? I MADE MY DEBUT IN** *VANITY* *Fair* with a photo taken on a cliffside in Telluride. I have my own stage-left box at the New York Metropolitan Opera. (Tom and Katie's is stage-right.) Three senators owe me favors. I have the oldest money there is, after Kate Winslet's and the Queen's.

# PART 5

# The Royals: English Nobility and Various Aristocrats
## (Like Me)

*If someone would just give me a title and a tiara, I'd have nothing to complain about. Well, besides all the other disappointments in my life.*

I'VE NEVER BEEN MORE GRATEFUL FOR THE American Revolution than I was the day Prince William married a commoner. That said, I would be an excellent royal. I look amazing in capes, and I've been practicing lifting small weights long enough that my scepter-wielding skills are well honed. This chapter will take a closer look at the royals worth fearing—or befriending, just in case.

## Prince William and Kate Middleton

**THERE ARE CERTAIN** events that entire generations remember. My father's contemporaries remember where they were for the moon landing and Bobby Kennedy's assassination; Tom himself refuses to admit he was old enough to have experienced those things. (You're fifty, Tom. Deal with it.)

On November 16, 2010, I was awoken at five a.m. by a call from my publicist. Normally when a publicist rings before dawn, this means you've been nominated for a Golden Globe or something, but as I hadn't submitted myself for anything, I was immediately suspicious. She informed me that, as I had long dreaded, Prince William had decided to go ahead and marry Kate Middleton. There'd been an official announcement and everything. The Queen said she was "absolutely delighted."

Although most people only became familiar with the future Duchess of Cambridge on that dreary, infamous November day, I'd been tracking her movements for years. Certainly I'd been aware of her relationship with the Prince, but I never imagined that, even in these modern times, the Queen would allow her grandson to marry a commoner. I'm certain that *I* have more royal blood than the Middletons.

Regardless of my concerns—or, I am sure, the concerns of the monarch, with whom I would like to one day discuss the relative merits of Her "Royal" Highness Catherine—they got married anyway. It's a nice thought, I suppose, that Prince William and Kate Middleton seem to actually love each other, though I've never had a problem with marriages of political convenience. Look at Diana and Charles (the early years) or Bill and Hillary Clinton or, you know, Tom and Katie Cruise, and you'll find that love matches are overrated, especially when it means marrying a working person.

On the one hand, I understood that sour little bridesmaid more than anything in the world. And on the other hand . . . what an ungrateful monster.

Why do Kate Middleton's life choices affect me so much?

Because she's like a ticking time bomb. One day, probably soon, she's going to have a baby. Who knows, by the time you sit down to read this book, she could already have given birth to a beautiful English rival, a baby girl who (thanks to a Commonwealth-wide policy shift) would one day rise to be Queen of England, regardless of the brothers who may follow her. If that is the case, and a young princess has already been born, thank you. Thank you for considering me relevant enough to read this book.

I live in constant fear of that inevitable day. Why else would I have built this panic room?

See, British royalty has always been powerful, but they haven't always been beautiful. Thanks to Diana, Princess of Wales, and Duchess Kate, the next generation of the monarchy will only really be one-quarter Windsor. Charles's genes will fade into oblivion. And she and I will both be powerful, and we will both be beautiful, but only one of us will be a princess. The injustices of the world are myriad, and they are painful. My only relief will be if she inherits the Duchess's working-class accent and the Duke's hairline.

In America, our political royalty is *earned*. The children of the President of the United States are thrust into a spotlight that most people are not ready for. For the record, I am ready right now to be a First Daughter. If given the opportunity, I'd be negotiating peace treaties from the Situation Room within the first week. Syria would be liberated, and the United States would have gotten France to agree to Most Favored Nation status, just because those import taxes on clothes and cheese are *outrageous* and completely not working for me.

Too bad my father is . . . my father.

## Chelsea Clinton

CHELSEA CLINTON IS most memorable as a First Daughter for going through an extremely public awkward period from age twelve to about age twenty-two. She proved, however, that phases end, and even the weirdest faces can triumph over adversity. After taking media heat for years, Chelsea graduated from high school and attended Stanford, Oxford, and Columbia, before having a big, fancy wedding and becoming an NBC contributor. Whether because of her many degrees or her unusual experience as a First Daughter, Chelsea has become more admirable as an adult than her political celebrity peers. One can hardly imagine that Bristol Palin or Meghan "Not Worth an Emoticon of Respect" McCain could have overcome the hardships that Chelsea has with such grace. I mean, even her crazy hair looks good now.

Honestly, the only thing Chelsea could do to make me like her more is to get Hillary to stop wearing scrunchies.

## Jenna and Barbara Bush

MEANWHILE, THE BUSH twins are best remembered for attempting unsuccessfully to use fake IDs while underage. (Jenna tried to pass herself off as "Barbara Pierce," as if using the name of a former First Lady wouldn't be a tipoff of any kind.) Jenna and Barbara have a pretty serious smart one/pretty one dichotomy going on, similar to that of Owen and Luke Wilson. It's almost like the post-White House personality of Chelsea Clinton got split into two, less awesome people: one, the fancy-wedding lamestream media-type, and another, the brainy progressive working lady.

Their fashion is, and always has been, pretty nondescript Washington blah-blah-business-casual. Which is why my favorite part of the 2008 Presidential turnover was the fashion revolution that happened at 1600 Pennsylvania Avenue ...

## Sasha and Malia Obama

**OH, THESE GIRLS. DOES ANYTHING MAKE ME PROUDER** to be American than the sight of these First Daughters in tweenage couture? Sure, Malia's going through a growth spurt that puts her in a height percentile matched only by Taylor Swift and professional basketball players, but once her features become proportional, she could be the first runway model-slash-astro-physicist. In addition to their sharp fashion sense, Sasha and Malia are both quite cultured.

When President Obama invited comedian Aziz Ansari to the White House, he said it was because Malia is a fan of *Parks and Recreation*. Although I generally avoid commercial network television, anyone who doesn't like Amy Poehler is immediately suspect. Unlike most famous children, I will support whatever life and career choices Malia makes—and you know I don't say that lightly.

Mostly, I would just like both of them to know that I'm available whenever they need help. I am very trustworthy with state secrets, and I look great in red, white, *and* blue.

## The Trumps

WE ALSO, OF COURSE, have another kind of royalty in America—the kind you buy. Donald Trump started a near-royal empire with ex-wife Ivana in the 1970s that now includes five babies—four grandchildren and one young son. Granddaughter Arabella (daughter of Ivanka) shows the most promise and seems to have the best head of hair of the bunch. I mean, look at this photo. Look which child Mr. Trump chose for the inaugural cover of *Trump* magazine.

When it looked as though Donald Trump might run for president, I was intrigued. I'm not sure about his social policies, but I know he wouldn't make me pay any capital gains taxes, so I probably would have voted for him. (Don't ask me how I vote, but let's just say I've cast at least one absentee ballot in every election since 2008.)

Even though my heart belongs (and is contractually obligated) to Cruz Beckham, I'd be willing to negotiate my way out of that one if it meant wearing a tiara. Call me shallow, but if it's a deal Grace Kelly was willing to make, then it'll work for me, too.

# WHO'S DOING IT RIGHT

LET'S SEE. I LIKED THE TWO LITTLE BRIDESMAIDS AT THE
royal wedding who neither made a scene nor were related to
Camilla. (I have a theory that every time someone calls Camilla
"Her Royal Highness," a bird dies.)

I also like Giulia Sarkozy, Former First Daughter of France,
but mostly because her parents, ousted French President
Nicolas Sarkozy and singer/actress/First Lady Carla Bruni,
never take her out. I assume Giulia lives a quiet life of dignified
exile in the British East Indies, like Napoleon, but with better
food. It's a little limiting, but it's good work if you can get it.
Also, as long as she's hidden away, she can't compete with me.
It's really a win-win situation.

Also, let us all remember that true nobility comes from our
hearts, not our genetics. My tiara and scepter may have been
sixth birthday presents from Tom, not passed down from
Queen Victoria, but the diamonds shine just as brightly. In
every way that matters, besides actual noble blood, I am as
much a princess as this country could ever need.

# PART 6

# Cliques
# I'm Not In

*It's rough in this town if you aren't in the right crowds, and I've learned precisely which ones have the best payoff in social capital, favors, and birthday gifts. (Hint: George Clooney's friendship comes with Italian villa access.)*

THIS TOWN IS NOTHING IF NOT CLIQUISH. YOU may have thought you were done with cliques when you graduated from your public high school, but you'd be wrong if you were involved in Hollywood's elite circles. Alas, there are a few Hollywood cliques I am not in; some of these I am comfortable avoiding (e.g., the one that involves Violet Affleck), while others remain frustratingly elusive to me.

# The Spice Children

*(Brooklyn, Romeo, Cruz, and Harper Seven Beckham, Phoenix Gulzar, Angel Murphy Brown, Madison Belafonte, Beau and Tate Jones, Scarlet Starr, and Bluebell Madonna Halliwell)*

**I'M SOMEWHAT IN THIS** one by proxy, as a frequent plus-one of Cruz Beckham's, but I will never be a full-fledged member, and that hurts me. Although somewhat of a joke while performing, their mothers have garnered respect in their retirement and have become legends. Isn't that always how it goes, though? Like Van Gogh or Vermeer, the Spice Girls just weren't appreciated in their

time. Anyway, all five Spice Girls now have children, and although Posh's are by far the most famous, they all share a unique friendship having been part of something so iconic.

I have to say, though, that some of the Spice children haven't lived up to expectations, and that has left this group as a bit of a mixed bag. The Beckham children have vastly exceeded their responsibilities to the respectability of the group, but some of the others aren't doing the Spice name any favors. The only others that you see regularly are Melanie Brown's, and that's only because she had a reality show. And Mel C's daughter, Scarlet Starr? Now there's a name with an implied career trajectory.

## Birdie Silverstein and Matilda Ledger

**THIS ONE MAKES ME MAD BECAUSE** I should be invited to their parties, but they choose to exclude me, even though they're Birdie Silverstein and Matilda Ledger, and I'm who I am. Right now you are probably sitting there thinking, "Who is Birdie Silverstein?" Maybe you are turning to your neighbor and saying, "Do you know who Birdie Silverstein is? Because I don't." And your neighbor probably said to you, "No, Muffy, I don't know who she is. Let's Google her." Well, you don't have to Google her, because I'll tell you. (Also, Google probably wouldn't turn up any results anyway.)

Birdie Silverstein is the daughter of Busy Philipps and some guy. (You can Google Busy Philipps if you don't know who she is, which is perfectly acceptable.) Matilda Ledger is the daughter of Michelle Williams and the late Heath Ledger. Matilda is famous because she inherited her father's beautiful face. (Beauty can be a tricky thing. Thank goodness I got

mostly Holmes genes in the face department.) Busy and Michelle are cute hipster BFFs. They are like twee-FFs. But do you know how they met?

*Dawson's Creek*, people. They are deliberately excluding me, the lame Van Der Beek kids, and the inevitably beautiful children that Joshua Jackson will have. I can't even benefit from Katie's trademark role in this town. The bottom line is, don't trust Birdie and Matilda. They use exclusion of their peers as a tactic to increase their own self-worth. Also, Matilda counts cards and *will* take your favorite earrings in blackjack. I learned that the hard way.

# Sports Families

*(The Woodses, the Breeses, the Bradys, and the Mannings)*

**I DON'T KNOW MUCH ABOUT SPORTS BEYOND TENNIS** and polo—the only activities I'll participate in that require sweating—but I do know that everyone who has ever won a major professional sporting event is part of an elite, uniquely American club. And when they marry a beautiful woman (usually a former supermodel) and have children, they're part of an even tighter circle—athletes with babies. There are four families in the sports world that are at the top of the heap.

The Woods family is, well, not really a family anymore, but they are still among the most famous. Forget about Tiger Woods (everyone else has); it's his ex-wife and children who maintain an elusive kind of fame. Elin Nordegren is pretty much the modern-day *First Wives*

*Club* all by herself. You know: she didn't get mad, she got *everything*. And then she tore the house to the ground just to show she could afford to.

She is my hero.

Sam and Charlie Woods, the children, are little enigmas. They live in Florida, a state with little to offer besides fast food chains and alligator attacks. But they are sitting on so much money that it doesn't even matter how often they are photographed; they'll be comfortably famous as long as the world remembers anything about 2010.

Drew Brees, meanwhile, is a football player (American football—not to be confused with Beckham football) for the New Orleans Saints, and has a reputation of being a real family man. One of the most famous images of Brees is of him holding his earmuffed son Baylen above his head after winning the 2010 Super Bowl. Honestly, Brees probably wouldn't have been named Most Valuable Player if his baby hadn't been so adorable. (The Breeses now have three children, because the first one was such a good investment.) Part of their charm, too, is their association with New Orleans, a dirty little southern city with mushy food and a decent comeback story. Those babies probably have southern accents and everything.

As a feminist, I feel it is my duty to explicitly hate Tom Brady and everything he stands for. He left actress Bridget Moynahan when she was pregnant with his baby, quickly coupled up with Brazilian supermodel Gisele Bündchen, and thereafter lost any hope of being friends with me. Tom now has son John ("Jack") Moynahan—you go, Bridget—and another son, Benjamin Brady, with Gisele. They're both extremely cute little boys, but you just have to wonder what their manners are like when their dad is Tom Brady. Gisele, also, is just the worst. She's been dinged in the press (and rightfully so) for suggesting that she birthed Bridget's son: "I'm so lucky to have my little munchkin [Benjamin], and I have two because I also have John," she told *Vogue*. She also got in hot water at the 2012 Super Bowl for claiming, after her husband's team lost, that his teammates had let him down. She's a real class act, that Gisele. I'm just glad she can't vote in this country.

Yeah, team Moynahan all the way.

And, finally, there's one family whose name is as valuable to athletics as mine is to fashion. (Although let's be clear: in the

grand scheme of things, they're still not nearly as valuable as I am.) Between them, Peyton and Eli Manning have three children: Peyton and his wife Ashley have twins Marshall and Mosley Manning (eh, I'm over alliteration), and Eli and his wife Abby have daughter Ava. (Fun fact: the cousins were born within ten days of each other. Yes, I know how to use Google.) What separates this family from, say, the Bradys is that they seem like genuine people; both brothers have known their wives since college, gave their children respectable (if somewhat southern) names, and have relatively low-profile (read: boring) lifestyles.

In conclusion, I'm not really jealous of or interested in marrying into a sports family. Worst-case scenario: your father becomes a national laughingstock and a shame upon your name. Best-case scenario: you're a nobody who has to live in Indianapolis or New Jersey. No, thank you.

## The Afflecks and the Damons

*(Violet, Seraphina, and Samuel Affleck, Alexia Barroso, and Isabella, Gia, and Stella Damon)*

**I'D RATHER EAT GLUE THAN SPEND AN AFTERNOON WITH** these people, which is why their little clique is so sad. Matt Damon and Ben Affleck have been friends since childhood and keep their families in close touch to this day. They vacation together, and it was rumored that the Damons were among the first friends to visit

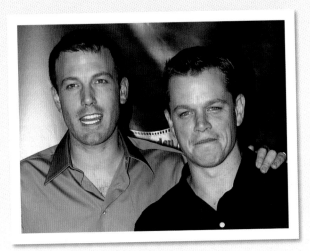

the Afflecks in the hospital after baby Samuel was born in February 2012.

Of all the celebrity families, these two definitely seem like the most (ick) "normal." (Well, except Ben Affleck. That guy is nuts.) Which is why I always wonder what they *do* on their joint holidays. I imagine it's a lot of, like, Yahtzee and healthy snacks. Maybe once on the trip, Jennifer Garner goes crazy and has two glasses of rosé. Damon and Affleck reenact their glory days by performing scenes from *Good Will Hunting*. Everyone's in bed by ten.

Yeah, these families don't invite me to things, but I'd probably pass anyway. I just enjoy fun too much.

# The Witherspoons and the Winslets

*(Ava and Deacon Phillippe, Mia and Joe Mendes)*

REESE WITHERSPOON ONCE SAID, "IMAGINE MY GOOD
fortune when Kate Winslet moved into my neighborhood, rang
my doorbell and said, 'Dahling, Sam [Mendes] is off shooting and
I believe our children are the same age. Could they possibly have
a play date and oh, by the way, it's almost nine o'clock and I've
had nothing to drink, do you have any wine?'"

See, you didn't even know that Reese Witherspoon and Kate
Winslet (and, therefore, their children) were friends, did you?
And now you are rearranging your life's priorities so that you can
be in their clique. Their children are therefore in one of the most
elite Hollywood castes of them all, built on true talent, lucrative
careers, and good hair genes. I can only hope they understand
how rare and special that is.

## The Poehlers and the Feys

*(Alice and Penelope Richmond, Archie and Abel Arnett)*

**WHEN AMY POEHLER** was pregnant with her son Archie, she told reporters, "I don't care if it's a girl or a boy, I want it to marry Alice Richmond, Tina's daughter. We'd make a lovely mother and mother-in-law of the bride." I'm not sure if it's working out romantically, but these four children of comedy are definitely in one of the top-notch celebrity cliques.

Tina's daughters look brainy but nice, and Amy somehow managed to produce a child so shockingly ginger, I'm thinking of starting a movement to track down his long-form birth certificate.

Abel's mysterious genes aside, these children are some of the most popular in the business. And, you know what, I get it. I don't understand why a lot of celebrity children are famous (Mason Disick, anyone?), but these kids deserve the occasional attention. I mean, Alice Richmond's humor is sharper than Shiloh Jolie-Pitt's snaggletooth.

## The Children of the Hollywood Gays

*(Zachary Jackson Levon Furnish-John, Harper and Gideon Harris, Matteo and Valentino Martin)*

**IS THERE ANY GROUP MORE EXCLUSIVE AND SECRETIVE** than this one? (Well, besides mine.) Recently, famous Hollywood gays decided they were feeling left out of the baby craze, and who could blame them? Why should, for instance, Anderson Cooper be excluded from any activity that Tori Spelling's done *four* times? Thanks to modern technology and the generosity of three well-paid gestational surrogates, the talents behind "Candle in the Wind," *The Smurfs*, and "Livin' La Vida Loca" were able to pass their genetic material down to future generations.

Zachary Jackson Levon Furnish-John—who is addressed by all five names at all times—is the long-awaited child of Elton John and his husband David Furnish. Elton, obviously, is a larger-than-life individual, with a long and storied career and a personality bigger than the castle he owns in the English countryside. (Actually, so far, this doesn't sound all too different from life with Tom Cruise.) But he is also of the old-school mindset that private life should be private, and therefore, Zachary Jackson Levon Furnish-John is rarely spotted out and about with his famous parents.

They did, however, take him to their annual post-Oscars party in 2012, which I was very jealous of. My father presented Best Picture, and I didn't even get an invitation. Just another reason that it pays to be in with this crowd, I suppose. I assume this is what Zachary Jackson Levon Furnish-John's life is like every day—surrounded by blue-haired pop stars and nineties sitcom actresses brandishing monkey cubs at black-tie parties.

Neil Patrick Harris and his partner David Burtka are basically the poster people for gay parenting. Their twins, Harper and Gideon, are impeccably dressed, always good for a cute talk-show anecdote, and just generally adorable. Also, at press time, their faces were still really fat. The Burtka-Harrises and the Furnish-Johns have been known to take yacht vacations together, further solidifying my belief that I was born into the wrong family. My parents still insist on *renting* yachts, as if we are some kind of family of paupers.

From the time his twin sons, Valentino and Matteo, were born (also via surrogate), Ricky Martin seemed to be living in a cutesy comedy where a handsome Latino has-been stumbles on two babies and must suffer the hysterical consequences. He doesn't have a nanny! He brings them backstage to his Broadway musical! They are friends with Oprah! It's all very modern. Unlike Zachary Jackson Levon Furnish-John and the Harris-Burtka kids, Valentino and Matteo are growing up with just one parent, which I have to say sounds pretty attractive. Not that I'd want that much alone time with either of my parents.

## The Cast of Mad Men

**THERE'S ONLY ONE NOTEWORTHY CHILD AMONG THE** cast—Kiernan Shipka, who plays Sally—but I mostly just want to be friends with everyone on the show (with the exception of January Jones, of course, who scares me). In lieu of personal friendship I would accept a cameo role, and I have a few suggestions for parts I could play, such as an heiress advertising her jewelry line, a young Caroline Kennedy, or in an Emmy-baiting departure from type, a classmate of Sally's from public school.

# WHO'S DOING IT RIGHT

**OF COURSE, THE BEST CLIQUE IS THE CLIQUE I AM IN—** the one that started around me. Membership is extremely closed, so don't get any ideas, Shiloh.

# Conclusion

S O THERE YOU HAVE IT. I HOPE YOU'RE GRATEFUL for these invaluable lessons. Maybe now you, too, can start behaving like an adult and dressing like you respect yourself. My greatest aspiration in life is to lead Hollywood's youngest generation into an era of Croc-less class. Is that too much to ask? It's not like Violet Affleck can't *afford* a Birkin bag. It's not like Willow Smith can't learn a little humility, get a Ritalin prescription, and calm herself down. It's not like Tori Spelling's kids can't . . . okay, okay. The Spelling-McDermotts might be a lost cause. You can't win them all.

But if this book helps even one person, or one person's underachieving child, improve his posture or wardrobe or table manners, I'll have done my part. (As if I haven't already. I mean, look at me.)

125 Conclusion

# Acknowledgments

I AM GRATEFUL TO SO MANY PEOPLE WHO HAVE helped me with this, a silly little thing that I am very proud of. (It's not as if Suri would ever say thank you, and somebody's got to do it.)

First, to Danielle Ballard, my conscience and my most welcome censor, thank you for telling me not to say that [redacted child] had a camel toe that day, even though she totally did. (And for every other judgment call.) I am lucky to work at a place like Penn Hill Group, where everyone has been almost unnecessarily supportive of my new night job.

Jordana Tusman, Chris Navratil, Amanda Richmond, Sue Oyama, Melissa Geller, and everyone at Running Press, thank you for taking a chance on me and Suri, and for being so patient and helpful.

To Anthony Mattero, my agent, your professional guidance has been the best thing about this year. I hope this makes you proud.

For everyone else who has offered advice and jokes, you are the best and funniest friends ever: Sarah Kupferman, John Krizel, Caitie Craumer, Chelsea Hagan, thank you. Annie Stamell, your encouragement means everything to me.

For my family, even though I am pretty sure you are only cool with this because I finally found a productive use for all of that knowledge about Jennifer Garner's personal life, I am very thankful for the support.

And, finally, thank you to the Cruises. Your daughter is a national treasure, but most especially to me.

# Photo Credits